Queen Lili'uokalani

CHERRY LAKE PRESS

Published in the United States of America by Cherry Lake Publishing Group
Ann Arbor, Michigan
www.cherrylakepublishing.com

Reading Adviser: Beth Walker Gambro, MS, Ed., Reading Consultant, Yorkville, IL
Book Designer: Jennifer Wahi
Illustrator: Jeff Bane

Photo Credits: © crbellette/Shuttershock, 5; © Hawaii State Archives, Liliuokalani,pre-1880, Photograph Call No. PP-98-10-009, 7; © Uploaded by KAVEBEAR/Wikimedia, 9; © Library of Congress/LOC No. 2017658685, 11, 22; © Brian A Jackson/Shuttershock, 13; © Uploaded by Jiang/Wikimedia, 15, 23; © Hawaii State Archives, Liliuokalani, 1890's, Photograph Call No. PP-98-12-010, 17; © Hawaii State Archives, Photograph Call No. PP-36-3-002/ Wikimedia, 19; © Hawaii State Archives, Liliuokalani,pre-1880, Photograph Call No. PP-98-13-015, 21; Cover, 1, 6, 10, 26, Jeff Bane; Various frames throughout, © Shutterstock Images

Cherry Lake Press is an imprint of Cherry Lake Publishing Group.

Library of Congress Cataloging-in-Publication Data

Names: Loh-Hagan, Virginia, author. | Bane, Jeff, 1957- illustrator.
Title: Queen Lili'uokalani / by Virginia Loh-Hagan ; illustrated by Jeff Bane.
Description: Ann Arbor, Michigan : Cherry Lake Publishing, [2022] | Series: My itty-bitty bio
Identifiers: LCCN 2022009926 | ISBN 9781668908884 (hardcover) | ISBN 9781668910481 (paperback) | ISBN 9781668912072 (ebook) | ISBN 9781668913666 (pdf)
Subjects: LCSH: Liliuokalani, Queen of Hawaii, 1838-1917--Juvenile literature. | Queens--Hawaii--Biography--Juvenile literature.
Classification: LCC DU627.18 .L54 20022 | DDC 996.9/027092 [B]--dc23/eng/20220415
LC record available at https://lccn.loc.gov/2022009926

Printed in the United States of America
Corporate Graphics

table of contents

About the author: When not writing, Dr. Virginia Loh-Hagan serves as the director of the Asian Pacific Islander Desi American (APIDA) Center at San Diego State University. She identifies as Chinese American and is committed to amplifying APIDA communities. She lives in San Diego with her very tall husband and very naughty dogs.

About the illustrator: Jeff Bane and his two business partners own a studio along the American River in Folsom, California, home of the 1849 Gold Rush. When Jeff's not sketching or illustrating for clients, he's either swimming or kayaking in the river to relax.

I was born in 1838 in the Kingdom of Hawai'i. I had many **siblings**. We were part of the **Native** Hawaiian **royal** family.

I went to **boarding school**. I loved music. I played **instruments**.
I wrote more than 160 songs.

What is your favorite subject in school?

I married John Owen Dominis.
We **adopted** three children.
He later became a governor.

I became queen in 1891. I was Hawai'i's first woman ruler. I was proud. A few months later, my husband died.

Who is your favorite leader?

A new **constitution** was put in place. It took power away from the Native Hawaiian people. I wanted to change this. I wanted to help my people.

The United States made Hawai'i into a **territory**. I fought back. I wanted freedom for my people. I tried to change laws.

I fought in court. I wrote letters to leaders. I supported my people.

I lost. I was jailed in my home for fighting back. I had to step down as queen.

I died in 1917. But my **legacy** lives on. Some of my songs are still sung today.

What would you like to ask me?

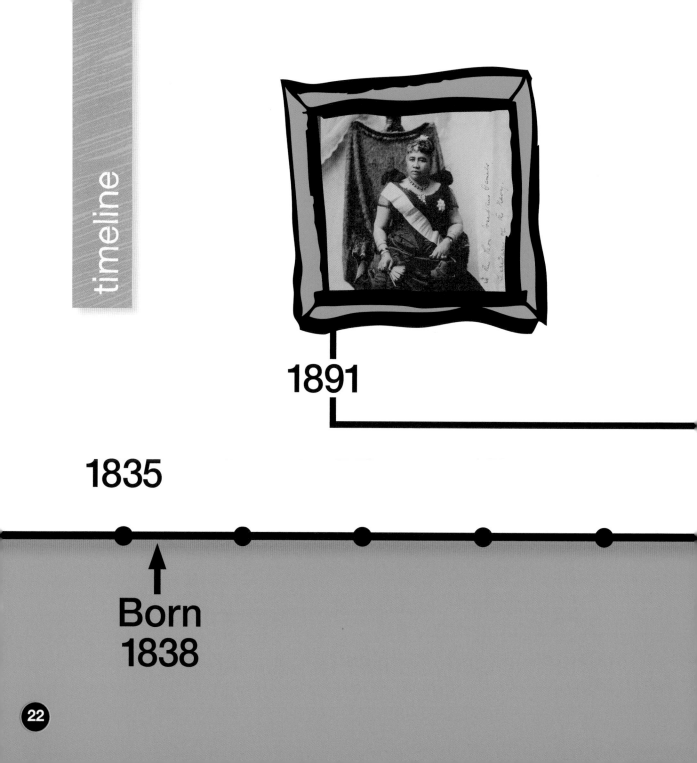

1891

1835

Born
1838

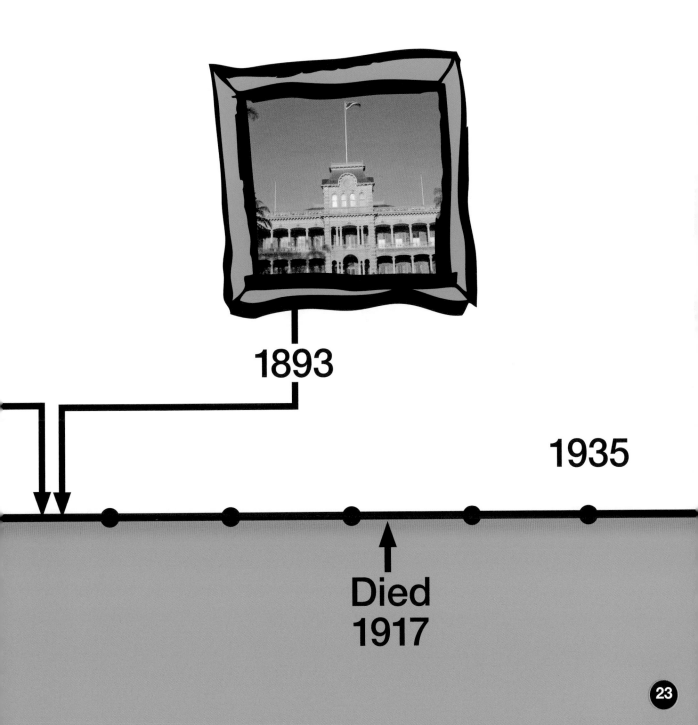

1893

1935

Died
1917

glossary

adopted (uh-DAWP-tuhd) legally made the son or daughter of someone

boarding school (BOHR-ding SKOOL) a school where students live full-time

constitution (kahn-stuh-TOO-shuhn) the basic laws of a nation, country, or state

instruments (IN-struh-muhnts) devices or tools that make musical sounds

legacy (LEH-guh-see) something handed down from one generation to another

native (NAY-tiv) born in a particular place

royal (ROY-uhl) a member of a ruling family

siblings (SIH-blings) brothers and sisters

territory (TER-uh-tohr-ee) an area of land that is controlled by another country or government

index